In and Out: Love Poems

In and Out: Love Poems

by

Arnold Johnston

© 2024 Arnold Johnston. All rights reserved.
This material may not be reproduced in any form, published,
reprinted, recorded, performed, broadcast,
rewritten, or redistributed without
the explicit permission of Arnold Johnston.
All such actions are strictly prohibited by law.

Cover design by Shay Culligan
Cover image from *Above the City* by Mary Hatch
Author photo by Sarah Matyczyn

Library of Congress Control Number: 2024950425

ISBN: 978-1-63980-666-9

Kelsay Books
502 South 1040 East, A-119
American Fork, Utah 84003
Kelsaybooks.com

For Debby, always.

Acknowledgments

I wish to acknowledge the following publications, in which the following poems have previously appeared, sometimes in slightly different form.

The Cumberland Poetry Review: "The Poet Visits Lake Michigan"
Embers: "Reduction," "Spectators as We Are," published to recognize my being a finalist in the 1990 *Embers* National Chapbook Competition
Encore Magazine: "Double Sonnet: Sunday Drive," "The Poet Has a Midlife Crisis"
The Fear of Drowning: a recorded compilation of Michigan Poets (Mad Queen Records, 1986): "These Lovers: *Amor Vincit Omnia*," "Contract Language"
The Infernal Now (Kelsay Books, 2023): "Love Token," "Cataracts"
The Malahat Review: "Contract Language"
New Poems from the Third Coast (Wayne State University Press, 1999): "Spectators as We Are"
Outerbridge: "Moon Goddess," "Double Sonnet: Sunday Drive"
Peninsula Poets: "A Shrine"
Rushing Thru the Dark: "Winter Dream"
Sonnets: Signs and Portents (Finishing Line Press, 2014): "Late Summer, Lake Michigan," "Double Sonnet: Sunday Drive," "The Poet Does Yardwork," "The Poet Has a Midlife Crisis"
The Weathervane: A Journal of Great Lakes Writing: "Spectators as We Are"
What the Earth Taught Us (March Street Press, 1996): "The Poet Visits Lake Michigan," "Double Sonnet: Sunday Drive," "Reduction," "These Lovers: *Amor Vincit Omnia*," "Moon Goddess," "Contract Language," "The Poet Does Yardwork," "Spectators as We Are"

Where We're Going, Where We've Been (FutureCycle Press, 2021): "Spectators as We Are," "The Poet Visits Lake Michigan," "Contract Language," "These Lovers: *Amor Vincit Omnia*," "The Poet Does Yardwork," "The Poet Has a Midlife Crisis," "Pantoum: Then to Now," "Radioactive," "Rainbow," "Sparrows," "Romeo and Juliet, from the Balcony," "A Shrine"

Contents

These Lovers: *Amor Vincit Omnia*	13
Moon Goddess	15
Reduction	17
The Poet Visits Lake Michigan	18
Contract Language	19
Double Sonnet: Sunday Drive	20
The Poet Does Yardwork	21
The Poet Has a Midlife Crisis	22
Spectators As We Are	23
Pantoum: Then to Now	27
Deborah, Always	28
Love Token	30
Radioactive	31
Rainbow	32
The Light That Guides My Way	33
Cataracts	34
The Heavens Turn	36
Romeo and Juliet, from the Balcony	37
Winter Dream	38
What the Earth Taught Us	39
Mall Dream	41
Sparrows	43
Pantoum: All We Cannot See	44
Anniversary Ghazal	45
A Shrine	46

These Lovers: *Amor Vincit Omnia*

They make us laugh. We see ourselves entangled
In their lifelines, analyze their brief
Collisions, feel with them the way to secret doors.
We celebrate their transformations, share
Their innocence, their faith in accident;
Their simple pleasure in their victories is ours.

They plan their assignations childishly,
Meet in places where their friends will see them;
Startled, they tumble breadsticks, spill red wine,
Duck their heads, two hunchbacks on a blind date,
Drawing all eyes to where their linked hands lie
Among the crumbs and stains. Everyone knows.

They weigh their options, all heavier than air,
Cite precedents, prepare their brief for love,
Brood for days on missed phone calls, their own obliquity,
Lie sleepless, anxious and absurdly proud,
Drop hints to wives or husbands, hoping
Someone will write an ending, find a cure.

They kill themselves or those they love; they tear
Their eyes out in despair and serve them
Sunnyside up to puzzled children robed
Like judges; leave shrill testaments to lust
Or vengeance and the blood's strong will; embrace
Their sin, distracted, as they lost their hearts.

They hold each other, cry like animals;
Their bodies' friction warms what need defines,
Makes ends remote and thought remoter still.
They, too, would watch in condescension,
But they're lost, as we might hope to be
If we allow our skin to dream their dreams.

The play goes on in all its acts and forms:
These lovers: their question: "Don't we beat all?"

Moon Goddess

She circles me, keeping her distance,
Knowing I'm under her influence, a little crazy.
My tides rise to her changeable aspects;
Her distant calm fazes me constantly.
Her face, the one she always shows,
Wears its beauty well; I never tire
Of that complex topography. But I want more:
I want to see her other side, the one
Our separate motions cause to be averted,
That puzzle only darkness can solve.
Her gravity is less than mine. And why not?
I'm heavier, take myself too seriously.
She thinks I see mystery where none exists.
She has forgotten, or ignores, the history
Or fantasy that draws us to each other,
The pull I feel inside, convincing me
That something tore her from me once,
Long before memory, and left an ocean
In her place, a deep familiar puzzle.
She seems content with larger laws—
What I can't live with, or without—
Knows the balance that holds bodies in place,
Foresees tsunamis, earthquakes, fumaroles,
All the lunatic foul weather of disturbed inertia,
Even the final plunge to where we both belong:
Together. The puzzle complete.
Explosion. Fireworks. Chaos. Oblivion.

Luna. The Earth. I flatter myself,
Exaggerate your beauty: it's too much.
We are ourselves, human, small.
No stars will tumble if our orbits merge.
And even should gravity prevail, if earth and moon
On some unlikely day fell free together,
We'd be among the millions blown sky-high,
No special fanfare, no soaring choir:
Little creatures here and gone.
But if it happens, as the last earthly
Fragments fly, I hope we're there together,
Declaring one our own, and celebrating,
In some old way, our new moon.

Reduction

*As a writer, one of your most important duties is to search your
dictionary for words appropriate to your message and audience.*
    —Kirkland & Dilworth, *Concise English Handbook*

You've brought me to a certain state,
Condition, arrangement, as to reduce
Glass to powder, or a person, perhaps,
To desperation, brought under control
Or authority. I'm an expression
Simplified; you've done it elegantly,
Adjusting by making allowances.
You've thinned the mixture by adding spirits.
In the process I've become less rusty,
Purer, closer to my elemental
State. When I'm with you, I'm simpler, my life
Less complex, too, as if something has slipped
Into place, restored, like a fractured bone.
And I, in turn, lessen your negatives
In density by slow development,
Maturing us into the haploid state,
Our own meiotic simplification,
Before we're both reduced at last, in life's
Good time, to our own absurd conclusion,
That proposition no one can refute.

The Poet Visits Lake Michigan

Hunkered, he's here beside her, picking stones
Along the wind-chopped margin of this lake
They've found their way to, where they've come to rake
Through memories like ash or blackened bones.
A lone fly bats his temples, backs off, drones
Away. He looks up, sees the lighthouse bake
Under the late summer sun. Will this make
A difference? Will it modulate their tones?
Or will they file away this weekend, chalk
Another try off the list as they edge
Their way to nothing? "Is it going to rain?"
She asks. Now they've come down to such small talk;
They shore up these civilities, a hedge
Against inflated hope, to keep them sane.

Contract Language

What price that woman's touch?
Anything within reason.
No. That's not the range we had in mind.

Outside, winter settles on the library,
The angled concrete paths; it clears the air,
Squeezes warmth out of standing water,
Freezes locks open, or shut, regardless.
You think of all the small deaths you've died;
They've taught you nothing of finality.
You know the value of a skid, how to
Steer into a dollar, why life imitates
Bodies, where some of the art is buried.
But you can't say why she, particular,
Discrete, catches in your mind like the end
Of breathing, why your knuckles, the hair
On the back of your hand, resurrect
The plane of her cheek, now, as you watch
Winter emptying the day.

You'd rip twenties into green snowflakes,
Fishtail and spin your way across Nebraska,
Dig up murdered legions and confess,
Hack continuously at time
With pen, brush, chisel, laser beam,
For that face, now, for that small death.

What's outside reason? My honor? My hope?
Now you're talking. We can do business.
Sign here.

Double Sonnet: Sunday Drive

On this late winter Sunday, on careful
Country roads, life slides by at forty-five.
Cold sunlight plates the hills gold as we drive
Past farmhouses in what feels like prayerful
Silence. Animals stand at rest where full
Troughs have called them. They scarcely look alive
In their calm indifference to us, who strive
So to keep moving. They stand immobile:

Spotted ponies, wool-thickened sheep, and great
Slow sows. Light stretches so taut and static
On the earth's curve, the road can't help but warp
Space and time by its motion, and we gawp
As through a boat's glass bottom, frenetic,
Alien to the quiet land's slow heartbeat.

Our transience must loosen shingles, scrape paint
From each farm we pass. The rawboned trees shake
Their wild hair. Spinster-like, they seem to ache
With condescension, and mutter their faint
Curse: they've seen it all before, and it ain't
So much, the living, the dying, the break
Of too many dawns, sudden cars that take
Pale, watching faces through this stillness, saint

And sinner. We look envious, they know,
And a bit tired, headed for a bad end,
No doubt, and driving faster than we should.
They know the signs and portents don't look good,
And favor no one, neutral, foe, or friend:
Each spinster lives to say, "I told you so."

The Poet Does Yardwork

The autumn air turns acrid with blue smoke
As flames take leaf and drifts of birds take flight.
He notes she's leaning on her rake, a sight
Inevitable as the years. The choke-
Cherry trees loose pits like buckshot. The cloak
Of green that shades the yard is gone; the bite
Of the north wind waits. He bags leaves, contrite,
A penitent who tried to shed the yoke
Of domesticity, the dominion
Of wedlock and good sense. Most nights he lies
Beside her now and listens to the clink
Of wind-chimes from the eaves; their opinion
Seems at such times the only truth. He sighs,
And turns to dream as some men turn to drink.

The Poet Has a Midlife Crisis

He lives now in a condo of gray brick
With a balcony that neighbors a tree.
This shows the consequence of making free
To choose new ways in middle age. Each tick
Of his wound heart reminds him how the wick
Draws light from the candle, how energy
Flares and fades as night outwaits day. No three-
Sided love wears patiently, yet he'll stick
At endings—always has—and take classic
Refuge in sleep from guilt and grief. But white
Noise, like tearing silk, arcs out of his clock
Radio, then a jingle for Vlasic
Pickles; and morning's comedy stirs slight
Hope of change: one more chip off love's old block.

Spectators As We Are

Sleet patters across my car's window
In the South Beach parking lot. Sitting
Here, hand in hand, we lament spring's slow
Sweep up the coastline from Chicago.

You're not sure I want to be with you;
You know I'm capable of running,
And you're angry. You point out how few
Years we may have, and I can't argue.

You press on: "We should think of each day
As the last gift we'll get." I'm nodding,
But I know we seldom find a way
To live our lives like that. And I say,

"We're never ready for disaster."
For even when we know what's coming,
Foreknowledge never helps us master
Our fate. Like the poor drunk bastard

At the local winefest; the bozo
Thought he'd end the night's fun by walking
Around the city parking ramp's low
Parapet. Falling, he said, "Oh, no."

Could it be he really didn't know,
Despite his friends' and his wife's pleading,
That he might plunge sixty feet onto
The dark pavement down there? And if so,

Can his brief fall convince us that we,
Ourselves, when life finds us performing
Our own crazy stunts, will probably
Feel the same thrill of surprise to be

Dying, too? How can it slip our minds,
Or can a part of us be lying,
That we forget how frail a tie binds
Us to the real world? What is it blinds

Us at such moments? Perhaps the sense
That we're immortal, or just watching
Our own lives, as if experience
Might be a TV show, more intense,

Perhaps, but no more real. Remember
The man who was videotaping
Skydivers, and who, as their 'chutes were
Blossoming below in the cold air,

Stepped out to join them? What the tape shows
Is the cameraman's realizing
That he has no 'chute. We know he knows
When he looks down and the picture goes

Crazy. As long as nothing is real
The camera's focused, recording
Everything; but when he starts to feel
For his ripcord and his veins congeal,

He spurns vision like a false lover.
And now we sit together, watching
Lake Michigan from the dry cover
Of my Toyota. Seagulls hover

Above the waves that attack the dock,
Neither birds nor gray water caring
About us or each other. We talk
Of all this, and of people who walk

Out on the pier to see the lake's show
Of power, despite weather warnings
And common sense. Now and then, we know,
Someone's swept away and sucked below,

Battered by the waves, and drowned. And I
Wonder if, when they find they're breathing
Water and know they're about to die,
They spend a moment wondering why

Their lives seemed like something they had paid
To watch, all the moments unfolding
Like someone else's story. "They made
The choices," you say. "They could have stayed

Where they were safe and warm. Whatever
They believed, life wasn't happening
To them. We make it happen. Never
Forget that. You can be too clever

On the subject, brood too much over
Whys and wherefores, and avoid choosing
Your own turning points: wife or lover,
Here or there. You know you can't cover

All the bets. You can't have certainty;
It's all a risk. There's no real knowing
Till you try. Some risks are bad, but we
Aren't one of them. So there." That's me

All over, as you know, spectator
And recorder, but seldom acting
For myself, habitual waiter
On eventual turns of fate or

Chance. So I'm the one I'm speaking of,
Who thinks life can be lived by waiting
For someone else to decide when love
Is over. My doubt goes hand in glove

With your certainty. And yet we lay
This morning on the beach, sheltering
Behind a low dune, watching the way
Snow formed brief stars on your coat. You'd say

It's the best image I could have drawn.
With that thought, I start the car. Nearing
The road, we glance back at the lake. One
Gull hangs there. You smile. And I drive on.

Pantoum: Then to Now

In cryptic images from alchemy
Jung saw a bridge from then to now,
A rainbow span, not the epitome
Of crackpot science and arcane knowhow.

Jung saw a bridge from then to now
In damn near every rendering
Of crackpot science and arcane knowhow
From art and physics all the way to the I Ching.

In damn near every rendering
Jung saw alchemy's power of transformation
From art and physics all the way to the I Ching;
And in the heat required for sublimation

Jung saw alchemy's power of transformation
In the creative force of love;
And in the heat required for sublimation
Alchemy and art work hand in glove.

In the creative force of love
The every only god makes certain
That alchemy and art work hand in glove
To help reveal what lies beyond the curtain.

The every only god makes certain
Our crackpot fancies and arcane knowhow
Can help reveal what lies beyond the curtain
And trace the alchemy of love from then to now.

Deborah, Always

Always Deborah,
Deborah when the day begins,
At the end of day, Deborah,
Deborah when it all began,
Like falling in a river,
Carried in the rush, Deborah.
A friend asked, "Did you ever
Try to swim ashore?"
Our only answer, "Have you ever
Fallen like that, been carried away?"
Love-drunk acrobats,
We found dactylic rhythm
In the moon-glow of cheap motels,
Deborah, Deborah, Deborah.
And when I tried to leave,
To opt for what I thought was sanity,
I had to take the train, because I knew
I couldn't drive myself without turning back.
But its dactyls would not stop muttering
Deborah, Deborah, Deborah.
And after a night of lying, denying,
The current now within,
What Plato told me,
What e e cummings certainly told me,
I threw myself into the morning train,
Its shining rails the current sweeping me back
To Deborah,
Deborah, mother and warrior, judge,
Bringer of peace,
Champion of women, Deborah,

Wife and lover, Deborah,
Artist and partner, Deborah,
Deborah, writer of the hard parts,
Tender of heart, quick to weep, Deborah,
Deborah, teacher and counselor,
Folk-singer's girl-friend, Deborah,
Beauty and survivor, Deborah,
Grave and frivolous, Deborah,
Irresistible current, Deborah,
Deborah, Deborah, Deborah,
Deborah when it all began
At the end of day, Deborah,
Deborah when the day begins,
Always Deborah.

Love Token

for Debby

I gave my love a necklace with two rings,
Her name on one, the other bearing mine,
Connected by a heart of gold that sings
Our love's sweet song in its unique design.
Her elegance is understated, plain,
Her dresses always black, setting the ground
On which the rings, the heart, the silver chain,
Remind us of the way our lives are wound
Together, inextricably. And when
I see her simple pleasure in this gift,
I know I've chosen wisely, and again
Those rings entwine my heart, my spirits lift.
It's just a token, but it stands for love
Like fingers sliding warm into a glove.

Radioactive

Inspired by *Soap and Juice,* Mixed Media piece by Ray Bacoskie, and "Radioactive," Lyrics by Imagine Dragons (Ben McKee, Dan Platzman, Dan Reynolds, Wayne Sermon, Alexander Grant, Josh Mosser, and Ben Linke)

All systems go, the sun hasn't died
Deep in my bones, straight from inside

She laughs and sings, "He's 'Radioactive,'"
As if the Dragons had imagined me.
She's hoping my core's become redactive,
Made sound by sounding, seeded, cancer-free.
The sound of laughter's what we need these days
To make sure that my inward juices flow.
Distraction is the soundest way to faze
Ill thoughts and tidings no one wants to know.
Soap and water, pills, to keep at bay
Post-op infection from the robot drill,
To make sure that I'm ready for the fray
With her who keeps me safe by force of will,
And sings, "Whoa-oh, he's radioactive.
Whoa-oh-oh-oh, he's radioactive."

Rainbow

After End of the Rainbow, *a mixed media piece by David Kamm*

A solitary dirtbird in pajamas,
He sits at his laptop playing solitaire.
She asks him if he plans to take a shower
Or sit in his grubby idleness all day,
Wasting time. The cards dance as he wins a hand,
And he tells her it's a possibility.
"Write me a poem," she says, and he concedes,
To himself at least, that he's been avoiding
The image of cartridge casings filled with crayons
Instead of bullets, loaded for art, lethal
To nothing except his hope to execute
The end of a rainbow where the urge to write
Might overcome the urge to kill. Poetry
Like the other arts, solves nothing, but it does
Remind us how much we'd rather live than die.
So what now? Another hand of solitaire?
He asks her if she'll join him in the shower.

The Light That Guides My Way

December 7, 2021

Your birthday's on the date of infamy,
But not because of you, who came after
By several years that cause for elegy.
In our lives this day gives rise to laughter,
Gifts, gratitude, for one more precious year
Together. Celebrating you and love
Is tempered now by just a tinge of fear
That in time's passage push will come to shove.
But what the hell—we're here and happy now,
Healthy as may be, and your beauty still
A light that guides my way and shows me how
To live with grace, wishing no other ill.
No infamy can mar our journey here;
We'll love our way through one more precious year.

Cataracts

1.

Drinking coffee at the Howard Johnson's
I overhear an old man behind me:
"I can't see. A cataract intervenes."
He says his eyepatch doesn't interfere
With sleeping, that he doesn't toss and turn
In bed, and that he always sleeps alone.
His woman companion commiserates.
He's grateful for her company, he says.
She says nothing. I watch them when they leave,
Note his tweed jacket, her pastel blue suit,
Hear her say, "Your fly is open, buster."
That happened almost forty years ago.

2.

Around that time, a friend said to me that
Our orchestra's Japanese-born maestro
Confided to him, "I have cataract."
My friend said, "That's too bad, Yoshi. Which eye?"
The maestro grinned. "Not in eye. Over there
In parking rot. Bland-new Eldolado."
Yoshi enjoyed playing his ethnic card.

3.

Now I'm probably older than the guy
In the Howard Johnson's, with cataracts
Parked in both of my eyes. My doctor's name
Sounds like an alias, though it isn't,
And he's teaching me about lens options,
Amblyopia, astigmatism,
And why they make for expensive choices.

4.

He removed my wife's cataracts last year.
I tell her my HoJo and maestro tales.
She says, "Forget Eldorados, buster.
You'll be fine. Dr. Doe will intervene
With a laser. And I'll make sure your fly
Is zipped up tightly. When it needs to be."

The Heavens Turn

December 7, 2022

The heavens turn; the Archer draws his bow
Above us as we take our little walks
Under the stars, knowing our status quo
Is fragile, subject to the thousand shocks
That flesh is heir to. But your birthday's here,
And soon we'll sit with friends and kin to mark
Our great good fortune that another year
Has found us still ascending like the lark,
Singing our songs and celebrating breath.
The day itself is cursed by history
For one dark act of infamy and death;
But every year I view it selfishly
As one more chance to thank the stars above
For one more precious year of life and love.

Romeo and Juliet, from the Balcony

Couples when new all feel the urge to touch
Each other as they walk from place to place,
Grazing, nudging, fondling, though not too much,
Lest friction lead to a full-on embrace
Before they're ready. But quite soon they'll be,
And then the touching will go on for years,
Or so they hope. For over time they'll see
Their hopes transmuted by their unwept tears.
We watch them walking on a small-town street,
He shuffling well ahead, and she behind
Five steps or so, intent on her own beat,
And no one knows what either has in mind.
We spy them from our balcony above
And thank our stars we're old and still in love.

Winter Dream

Our son drives us along a snow-clogged track
And slides amid a blinding swirl of white.
The journey ends within a *cul-de-sac*
When the car strikes a sign that, like a kite,
Rises and tumbles before us. The snow
Is axle-deep. He goes for help the way
We came, while you start off, careful and slow,
Toward a stand of evergreens. I stay
Beside the car and read the makeshift sign,
Scrawled with the owner's blunt and misspelled plea
For drivers to respect his borderline.
I peer through the feathery swirl and see
You standing near a stunted evergreen
That shivers off its white shroud, letting go
A scarlet cardinal, his crest unseen
Beneath a tiny cap of dazzling snow.
The small bird trembles like a sacred heart.
And holding hands we watch as day grows late,
The wind blows cold; and hoping not to part,
We face the night together, and we wait.

What the Earth Taught Us

An hour or so south, you told me, we could find
Sharks' teeth within the Mesozoic sludge
Dredged out along the banks of the canal.
These days, you hunt through stones and sediment,
Clip news from Olduvai; I try to write.
But I know the game: though paper may envelop
Rock, scissors will have their way.
And now a freighter slides by like a small
Norwegian town as we lie here and read
The ground, prostrate, nearsighted penitents,
Cautious students of our own earth; close study,
As you tell me, the only way to see.

Myopic, we note small things: slate wafers,
Crumbs of burnt cork, brittle slivers of old wood,
Glass shards. Red ants and jumping-spiders move
Among islands of stubble in the sand.
Your body lies near me under a sky
That hurts to look at. We focus on the ground.

I lost my Scripto ballpoint days ago
And haven't written since. What can I hope
To find here, if I'm so blind at home?
Keep looking, you say, smiling, levered
On your elbows, sand grains in the hollow
Of your neck.

                But my ears are keen: I hear
Your husband's pen scratch legal pads eighty
Miles north.

                    I find a tooth: smooth, gray-white,
Nearly perfect; sharp edged, of course. No need
To ask if this is shark, that nagging ache
In the world's dim memory.

You find a tooth.
I think of their tearing bloody clouds
And hunks from swimmers less well-versed, who left
No descendants to sniff for flesh in
Coastal shallows. Extinct: what sharks aren't,
Whose fossil teeth look newer than my own.

We find a necklaceful among the sand
And small debris. You always knew we would.
At every dredging-site, you tell me,
New searchers for the past appear. They know
You can't dig that deep without finding something.
And you look at me:

                    the day breathes out.
Neighbor. Friend. Woman.

                    And I nod. You're right.
I feel us gliding in the shallows,
Notice that your smile is new, and pocket
My shark's tooth, hard fragment of this day,
Wrapped hopefully in paper against
Its dredged-up, ancient, sharp insistence.

Mall Dream

I'm walking on the downtown shopping mall, looking for nothing in particular, passing souvenir shops, clothing stores, coffee shops, candy stores, barely glancing at the wares in their windows. The weather is neither hot nor cold. I'm wearing a light overcoat over a shirt and trousers.

As I stroll along I pass a young woman in her late twenties, dark hair to her shoulders, sensibly but stylishly dressed, holding the hand of what must be her daughter, a girl of four or five. Walking next to her is a woman of about fifty, who must be her mother or mother-in-law. She's dressed in a fashionable coat, hair professionally coiffed, and trailing a nimbus of expensive, somewhat sharp perfume. I vaguely sense a proprietary attitude in her regard for the younger woman and her daughter and move on to enter a nearby bookstore, where I browse for a bit and finally buy a new paperback translation of Chekhov's *Three Sisters,* perhaps affected by my mild curiosity about the two women and the little girl.

After leaving the bookstore I idle for a bit on the sidewalk, feeling the negligible weight of the book in my coat pocket. Then, still without purpose, I enter at the revolving door of the mall's remaining department store and, seeing the elevator doors slide open, I head toward it behind a female figure whose characteristics I barely register. As I reach the threshold of the elevator, causing the doors to pause in the open position, the woman turns to face me.

It's the young mother from the mall, without her daughter or the older woman. She steps forward, almost touching me, and I see that her brown hair frames a pretty oval face with an aquiline nose and wondering dark eyes. Before I can react, she places her hands on my shoulders and reaches up to kiss me on the lips, a kiss that's long and deep but without urgency or evident passion. She smells fresh, of lilac and shampoo.

At last she moves away and, looking up at me with those wondering eyes, says, "I want this."

I step back out of the elevator and say, "Don't wait too long."

The doors slide shut on her dark gaze. After a moment, feeling dazed, I turn and walk back toward the store's exit. I reach the revolving door at the same time as the older woman and the little girl, who are entering the store. As we circle each other in our separate spaces, they look at me without curiosity and are gone, leaving me on the sidewalk. Feeling bereft, I register the sharp scent of the older woman's perfume.

The mall whirls around me, and I think, "Who am I?"

Sparrows

I.

Sparrows
like feathered mice
mate on our balcony.
She seems detached from the process,
but he
flutters above her tail, engaged
by the imperatives
of their nature
and ours.

II.

Flowers on the patio
Sheltered from the autumn breeze
Sparrows flying to and fro
Flowers on the patio
Won't last long, the sparrows know
Soon November nights will freeze
Flowers on the patio
Sheltered from the autumn breeze

III.

On the balcony
A sparrow, feathers fluffed out,
Ready for winter.
Watching from my warm sofa,
I wish I could say the same.

Pantoum: All We Cannot See

The galaxies fly from us endlessly
As we concoct our little schemes down here.
The universe is just what we can see
From our own vantage points both far and near.

As we concoct our little schemes down here,
Like birthday parties for the ones we love,
From our own vantage points both far and near,
They all unfold beneath the stars above.

Like birthday parties for the ones we love,
We need to celebrate familiar things
That all unfold beneath the stars above
Regardless of black holes and quantum strings.

We need to celebrate familiar things,
Our love and your appearance in the world,
Regardless of black holes and quantum strings
And everything the Big Bang has unfurled.

Our love and your appearance in the world,
Though galaxies fly from us endlessly
With everything the Big Bang has unfurled,
Mean more to us than all we cannot see.

Anniversary Ghazal

for Debby

What's the matter with dark matter? you may wonder,
But answer comes there none, not whisper nor thunder.

We face each day anew, you and I, creating
What we can, despite the tendency to blunder.

Years go by, anniversaries accumulate,
While relationships around us fly asunder.

The universe throws quantum particles or waves
Apparently not by chance, the Big Bang's plunder.

Perhaps the only true dark matter is our love,
Lit improbably by the sun we age under.

A Shrine

A shrine to you sits on the seven-drawer
Chest in our bedroom in this resort town,
Photos slipped into the twists of metal
Monkeys' tails, your younger selves all looking
At me as I pick socks and underwear
From the drawers below. Before the photos
Lake stones sit, smooth Devonian corals,
Petoskeys, Charlevoix stones, crinoids, chert,
Reminders that our time here is no more
Than a fraction of what's gone before us.
A wallet-size of you at seventeen
Smiles down front, forever beyond my reach,
Although you're showering just steps away.
We met in your fourth decade and my fifth,
And we agree that if that seventeen-
Year-old beauty and I had been lucky
Enough to cross paths back then in our youth,
We'd have been a love story ever since.
I'll never hold that young girl in my arms,
But still I get to hold her every day;
And we know that whatever the lake leaves
On the shore for us to find, whether it's
Coral, beach-glass, or pebbles, you and I
Will search together, when at last we go.

About the Author

Arnold Johnston lives in Kalamazoo and South Haven, MI. His poetry, fiction, non-fiction, and translations have appeared widely in literary journals and anthologies. His plays, and others written in collaboration with his wife, Deborah Ann Percy, have won over 300 productions and readings, as well as numerous awards and publications across the country and internationally; and they've written, co-written, edited, or translated over twenty books, their most recent being *The Old Fart Plays*, just out from Dramatic Publishing Company.

Arnie's recent books are *The Infernal Now* (poetry, Kelsay Books, 2022); *Where We're Going, Where We've Been* (poetry, FutureCycle Press, 2020); *Swept Away* (novel, Atmosphere Press, 2021); and *Mr. Robert Monkey Returns to New York* (a collaboration with Debby, Brandylane Publishers, 2021). His other books include two poetry chapbooks, *Sonnets: Signs and Portents* and *What the Earth Taught Us*; *The Witching Voice: A Play about Robert Burns; Of Earth and Darkness: The Novels of William Golding;* and *The Witching Voice: A Novel from the Life of Robert Burns.*

His many English versions of Jacques Brel's songs have appeared in musical revues nationwide and on his CD, *Jacques Brel: I'm Here!* Arnie and Debby's award-winning one-act "Steering into the Skid" has had over 100 readings and productions nationwide and appears in *The MemoryCare Plays* (2014), an anthology of plays about Alzheimer's disease. Their AIDS-related one-act "Love Is Strange" appears in *Art & Understanding: The Twentieth Anniversary Anthology* (2015). From 2009–2012 they were joint Arts and Entertainment columnists for the award-winning national quarterly journal *Phi Kappa Phi Forum*. A performer-singer, Arnie has played many solo concerts and over 100 roles on stage, screen, and radio. He is a member of the Dramatists Guild, Poets & Writers, the Associated Writing Programs, and the American Literary Translators Association.

He was chairman of the English Department (1997–2007) and taught for many years at Western Michigan University, where he co-founded the creative writing program and founded the playwriting program. He is now a full-time writer.

Find out more at:
Johnston-Percy-Writers.com

www.ingramcontent.com/pod-product-compliance
Lightning Source LLC
Chambersburg PA
CBHW031207160426
43193CB00008B/534